American Patriotic Tunes
for String Ensemble

Arranged by **Robert Gardner**

Designed for a wide variety of settings and for students of different ability levels, the fourteen familiar patriotic songs in this single resource provide repertoire for formal school concerts and for informal performances at ceremonies or community events such as banquets or festivals. They can be used by any combination of bowed stringed instruments, from duets, trios or quartets, all the way up to a large string orchestra. All the pieces except "The Star Spangled Banner" and "Semper Fidelis" are designed to be repeated as many times as desired. Players may switch parts to make different arrangements of the songs. The score contains sample ideas for new arrangements.

Contents

Alfred Music Publishing Co., Inc.
16320 Roscoe Blvd., Suite 100
P.O. Box 10003
Van Nuys, CA 91410-0003

alfred.com

Copyright © 2011 by Alfred Music Publishing Co., Inc.
All rights reserved. Printed in USA.

ISBN10: 0-7390-7923-9
ISBN13: 978-0-7390-7923-2

America

(My Country, 'Tis of Thee)

Samuel Francis Smith
Arranged by Robert Gardner

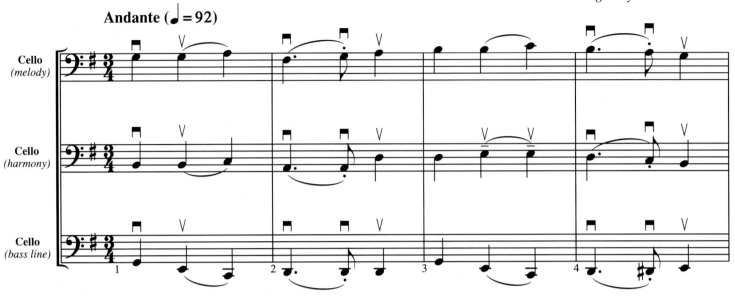

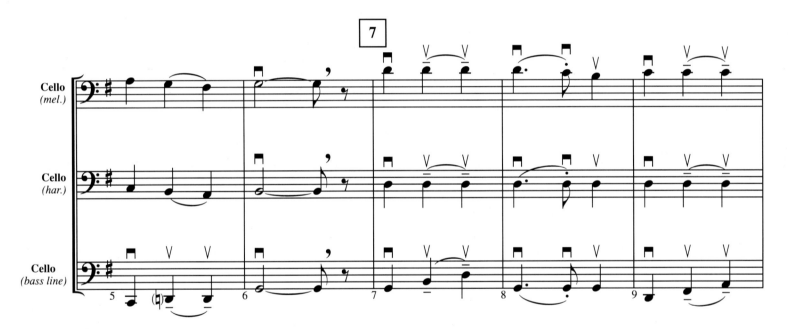

*Repeat the entire piece as many times as necessary.

America the Beautiful

Samuel Ward and Katherine Lee Bates
Arranged by Robert Gardner

*Repeat the entire piece as many times as necessary.

When Johnny Comes Marching Home

Patrick Gilmore
Arranged by Robert Gardner

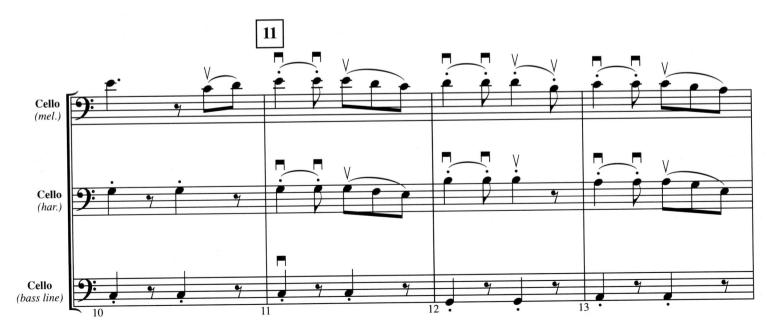

*Repeat the entire piece as many times as necessary.

The Star Spangled Banner

John Stafford Smith and Francis Scott Key
Arranged by Robert Gardner

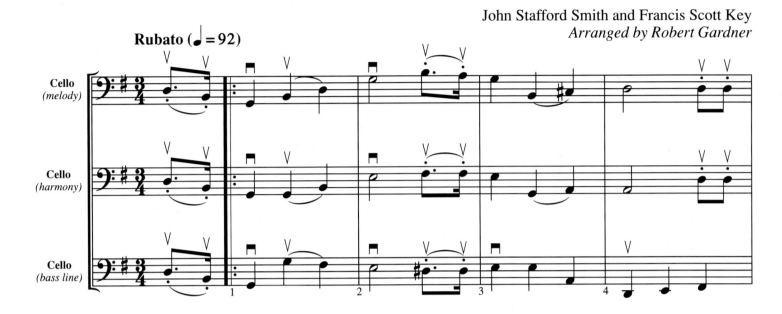

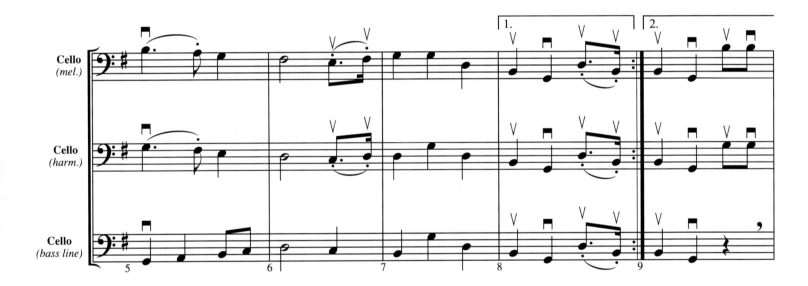

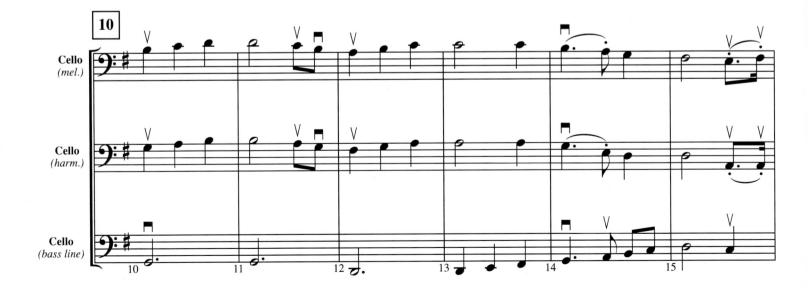

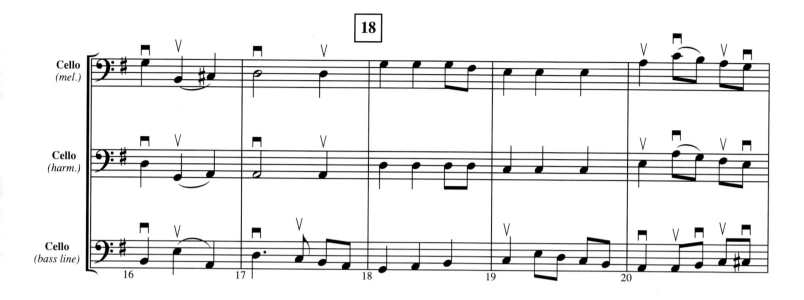

Over There

George M. Cohan
Arranged by Robert Gardner

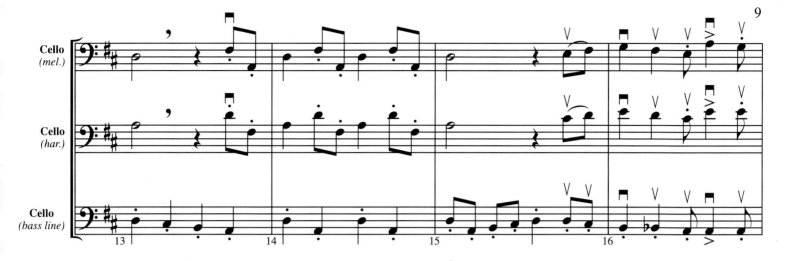

*Repeat the entire piece as many times as necessary.

The Army Goes Rolling Along

Edmund Gruber and Harold Arberg
Arranged by Robert Gardner

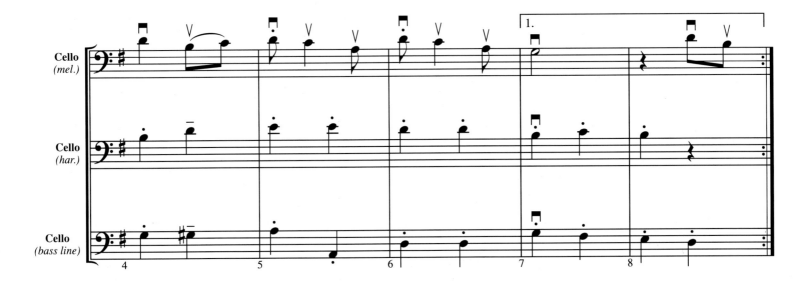

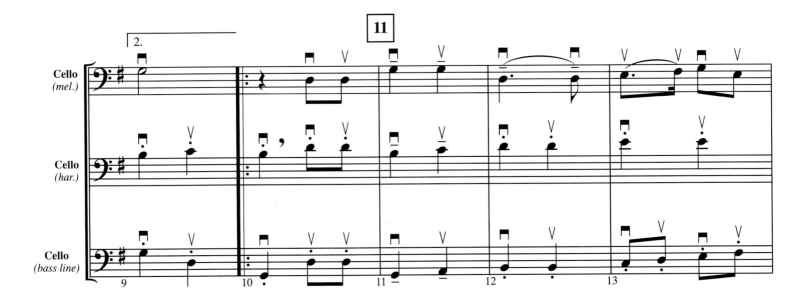

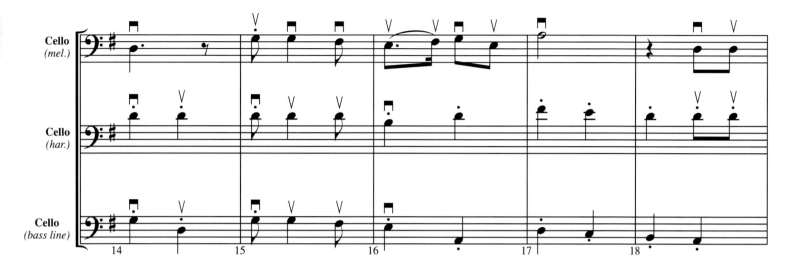

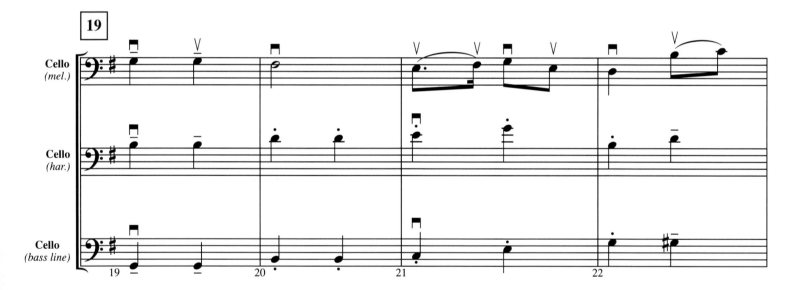

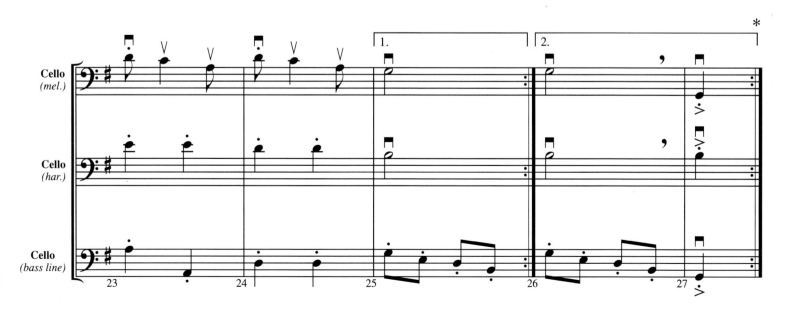

*Repeat the entire piece as many times as necessary.

Battle Hymn of the Republic

William Steffe and Julia Ward Howe
Arranged by Robert Gardner

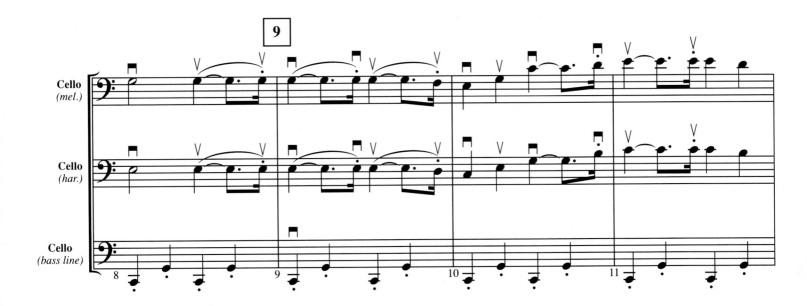

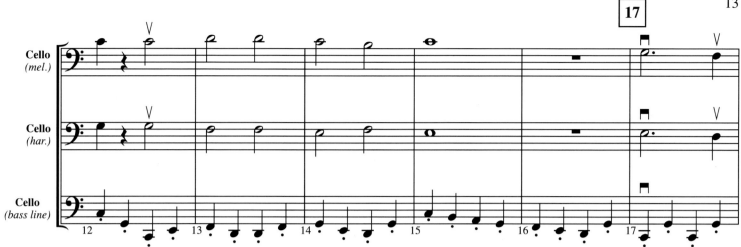

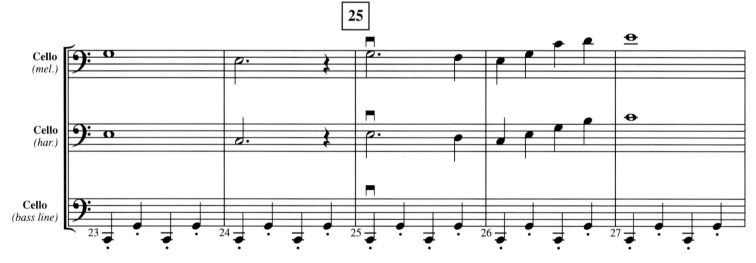

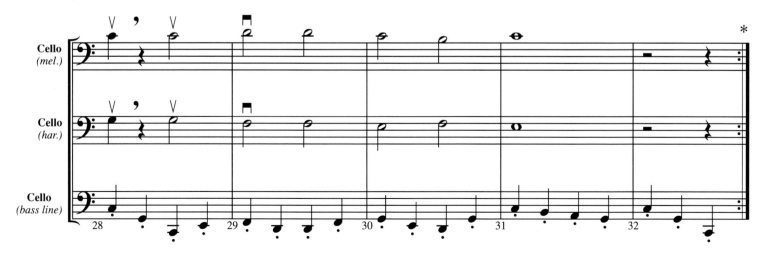

*Repeat the entire piece as many times as necessary.

Marines' Hymn

Jacques Offenbach
Arranged by Robert Gardner

18

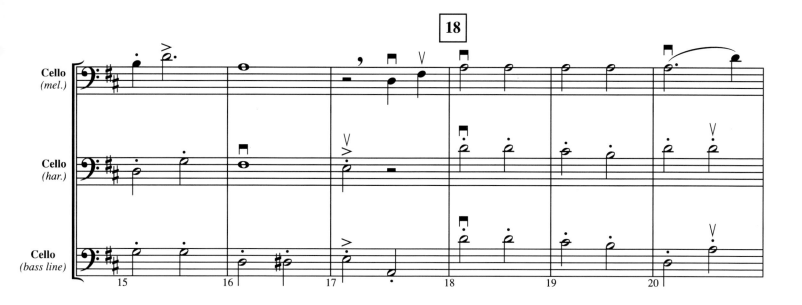

*Repeat the entire piece as many times as necessary.

Battle Cry of Freedom

George Root
Arranged by Robert Gardner

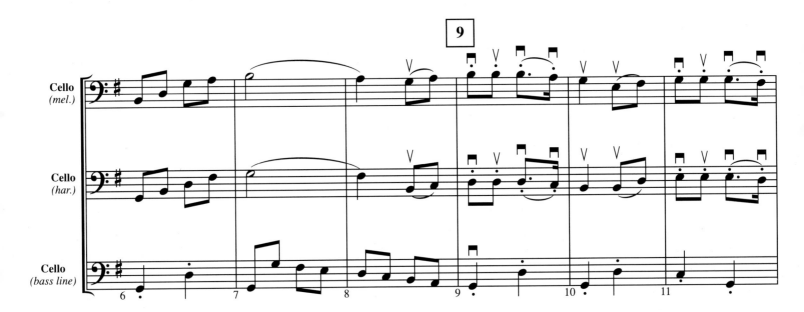

*Repeat the entire piece as many times as necessary.

The Yankee Doodle Boy

George M. Cohan
Arranged by Robert Gardner

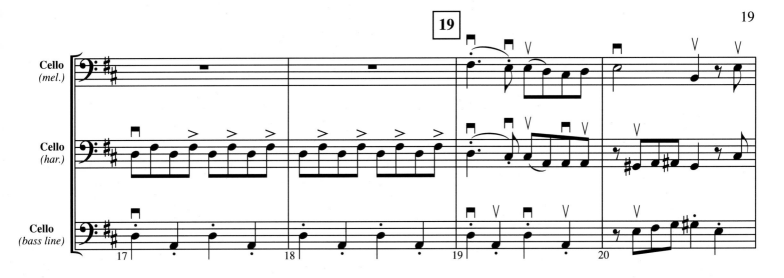

*Repeat the entire piece as many times as necessary.

Columbia, the Gem of the Ocean

Thomas Becket
Arranged by Robert Gardner

*Repeat the entire piece as many times as necessary.

American Patrol

Frank Meacham
Arranged by Robert Gardner

Stately march ($\textstyle\frac{1}{2}$ = 112)

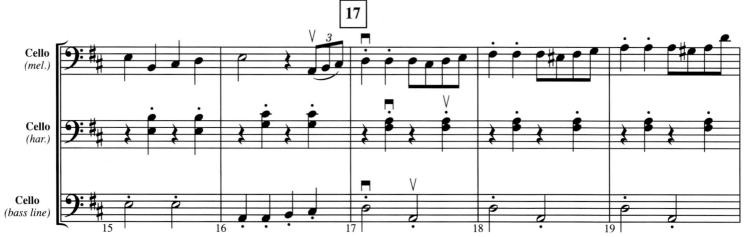

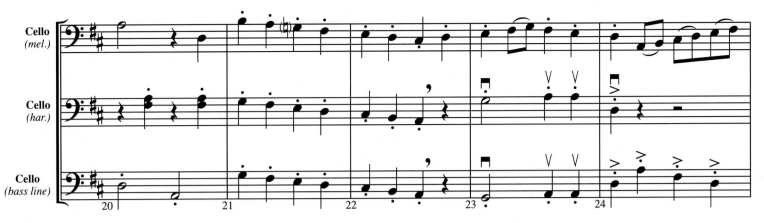

*Repeat the entire piece as many times as necessary.

You're a Grand Old Flag

George M. Cohan
Arranged by Robert Gardner

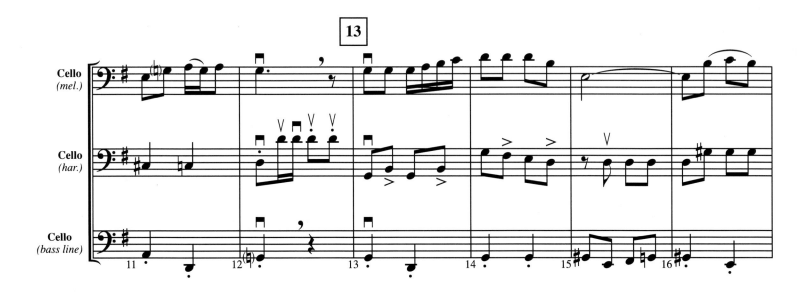

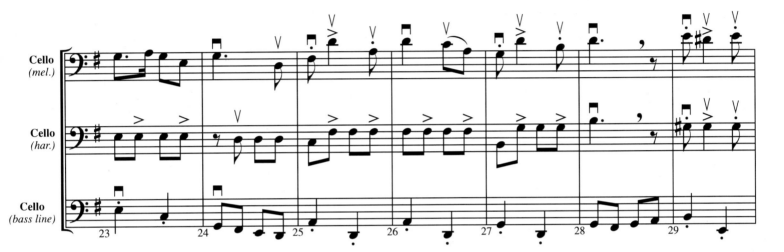

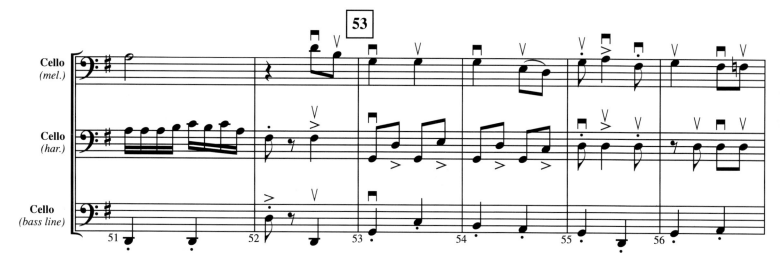

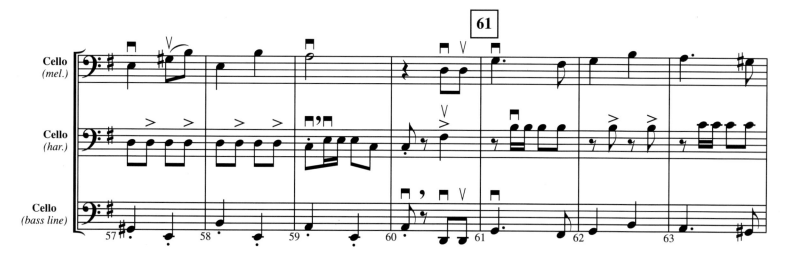

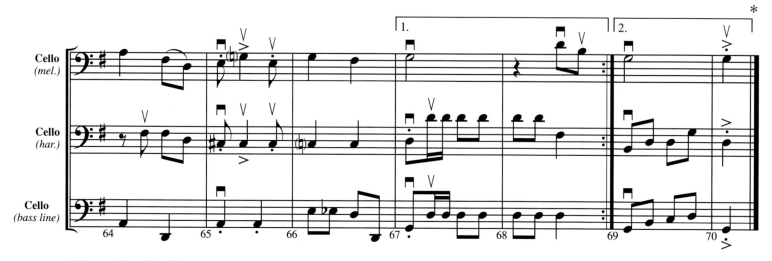

*Repeat the entire piece as many times as necessary.

Semper Fidelis

John Philip Sousa
Arranged by Robert Gardner

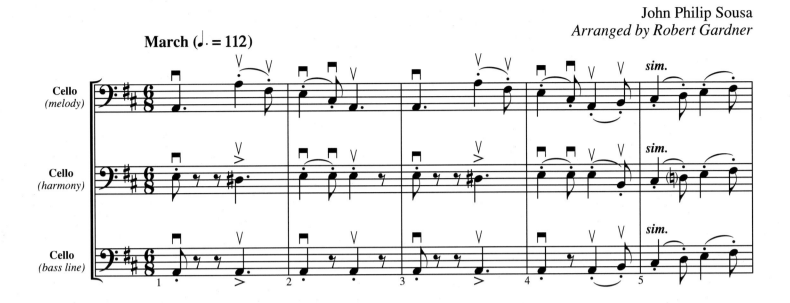

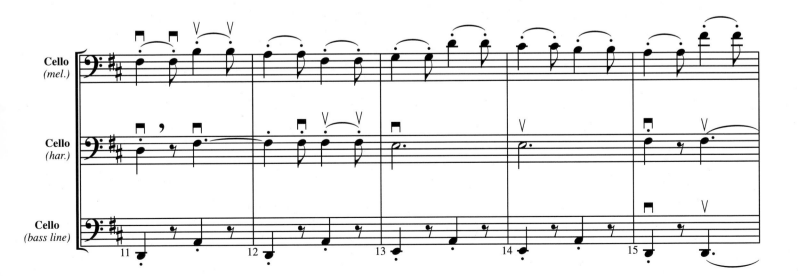

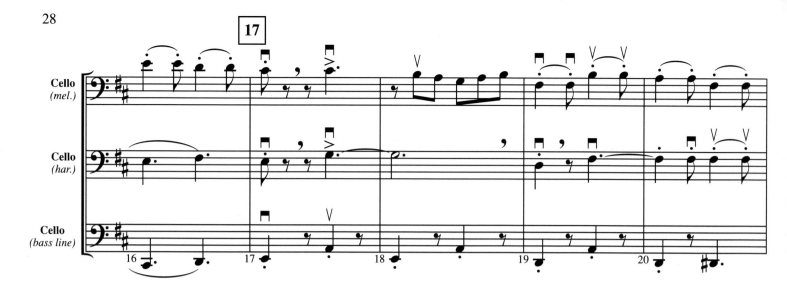

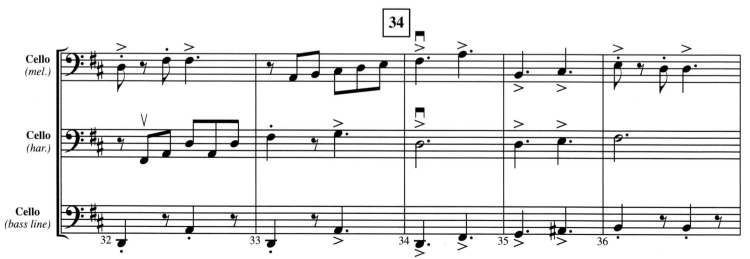

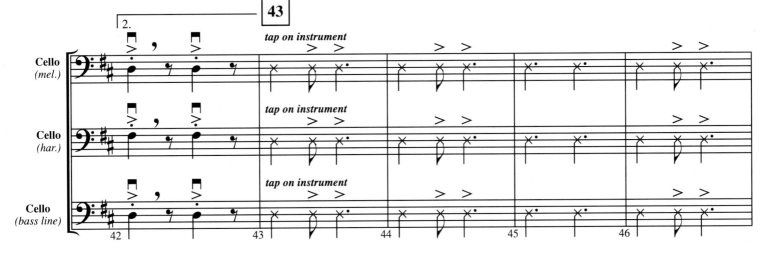

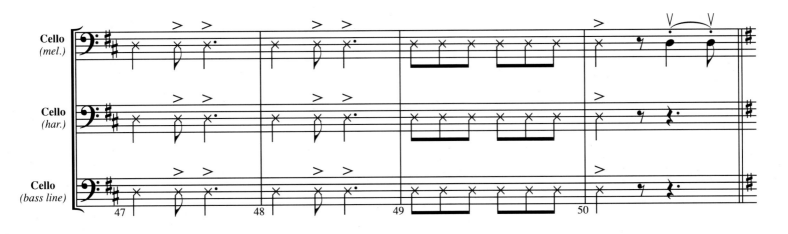

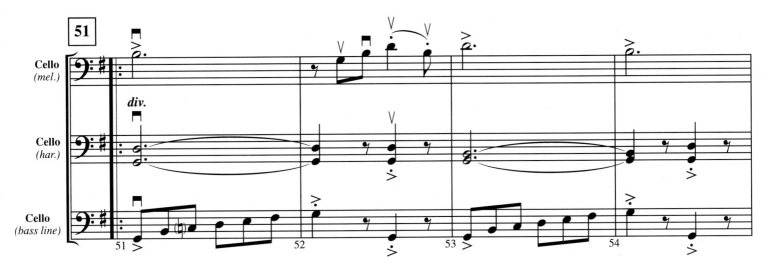

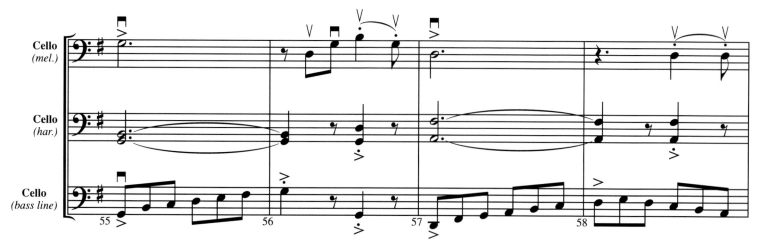

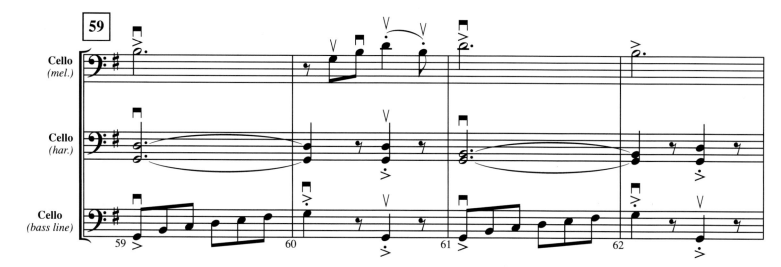

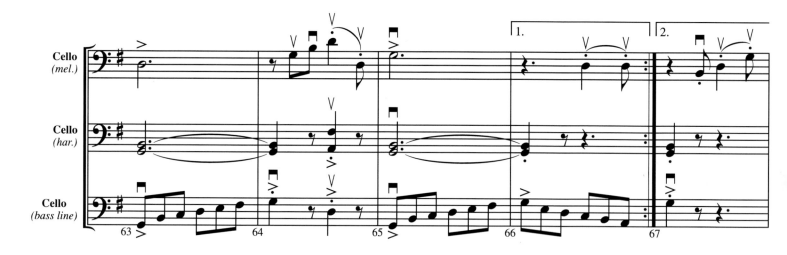

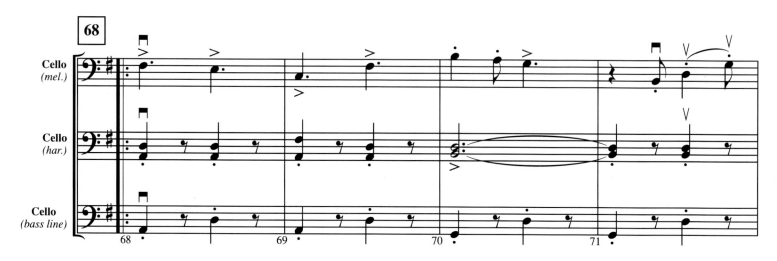

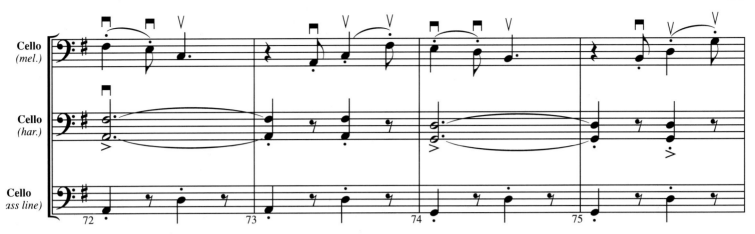

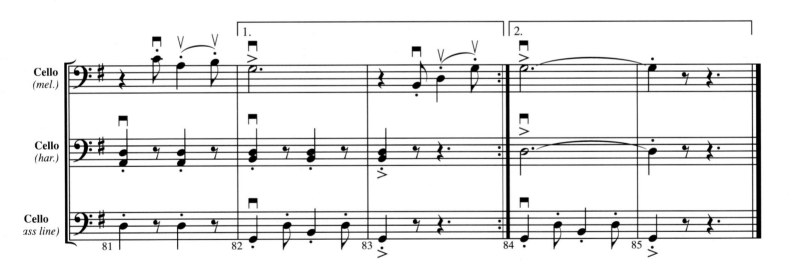

About the Author

Robert Gardner is a double bassist, conductor and composer with experience in a wide variety of musical genres. He has served on the faculty of the Penn State School of Music since 2003, where he is an assistant professor of music education, specializing in stringed instrument playing and teaching, alternative styles for string ensembles, and orchestral conducting.

His research has focused on the nature of improvisation and composition, as well as the supply and demand of American public school music teachers. Robert holds degrees from the Ohio State University and the Eastman School of Music. He has served as chairperson of the ASTA Alternative Styles Task Force, as well as Immediate Past-President of PADESTA.